Legacy
BUILDERS

2 Timothy 2:2

R O D   O L S O N

D E D I C A T I O N

I wish to dedicate this book to the Master
Coach and architect of my life, my Lord and
Savior Jesus Christ. The principles he left us are
truly timeless and life changing. I would also
like to thank my wife, Marla for all her patience
and love as a coach's wife and mother. This
book would not have been possible if not for
the vision of Frosty Westering, the ministry of
Scotty Kessler and Wes Neal, the steadfastness
of Kirk Talley and the unselfishness of Johnny
Square. I would also like to thank Derek
Fullmer and the Colorado FCA staff for all their
prayers and support. Finally, I want to thank
the Air Force football staff for their inspiration
and all the coaches and their spouses that we
have known over the years...this is for you.

Legacy Builders

Rod Olson

ISBN 1-929478-58-5

Cross Training Publishing
317 West Second Street
Grand Island, NE 68801
(308) 384-5762

This book is manufactured in the United States of America.

Library of Congress Cataloging in Publication Data in Progress.

Contents

GROUP COVENANT

I, _____

Commit with my Legacy Builders group to do the following:

1. Complete the Legacy Builder worksheet each week before the group session.
2. Pray regularly for my fellow group members.
3. Participate in all group sessions unless urgent circumstances beyond my control prevent my attendance.
4. Participate openly and honestly in the group sessions.
5. Keep confidential any personal matters shared by others in the group.
6. Be patient and compassionate with my fellow Christian coaches and my school as we grow closer to God and see how He wants us to serve.
7. I will pray for my school, my staff and my players at least one time per week.

OTHERS YOU WILL BE COMMITTING TO PRAY FOR:

_____
_____
_____

Signed:_____

Date:_____

LEGACY BUILDER GROUP MEMBERS:

_____
_____
_____
_____
_____
_____

Outline

Week 1 —What's in your Box?—Colossians 3:23-25
"What is the No. 1, central motivating factor in your life?"
➤ The purpose of this lesson is to help the coach learn what is truly driving his or her life.

Week 2—Are you F.A.T.?—John 14:1-7
"Who we are, where we are going, and how are we going to get there?"
➤ This lesson will help the coach remember who they are in Christ and what it means to be a Christian.

Week 3 —Get Wired—John 15:5
"Are you a Christian-coach or a Coach that is a Christian?"
➤ The purpose of this lesson is to assess where you are as a coach both in and out of the athletic arena.
CROSS REFERENCE: Romans 8:28

Week 4—The Traits of a Legacy Builder—Titus 3:1-2
"What it takes to be the Real-Deal!"
➤ This lesson will focus on being a servant, messenger and "a sent one." We will embrace the fact that in order to be the greatest, you must become the least.
CROSS REFERENCE: Mark 10:43-45

Week 5—Commitment to Excellence—Matthew 6: 19-25
"What are my goals and how do I reach them?"
➤ The purpose of this lesson is to discern Godly goals from worldly goals for a Christian coach, and to help the coach understand how to reach and measure those goals.
CROSS REFERENCE: Colossians 3:23-24

Week 6—Feeding the Monster—Matthew 25: 14-30
"Is the job eating you up...reset your priorities!"
➤ This lesson will focus on time management. We will discuss what a Christian-coach's priorities look like and how a coach can maintain balance within a hectic schedule.
CROSS REFERENCE: Matthew 6: 33-34

WEEK 7—TAMING THE TONGUE—JAMES 3: 1-12
"Living a coach's lifestyle...the way God wants!"
➤ The purpose of this lesson is to help the coach 'talk the talk & walk the walk' of a Christian-coach on a daily basis.
CROSS REFERENCE: Ephesians 6:10-20

WEEK 8—SEED PLANTERS—PROVERBS 22:6
"Kids may not listen to parents or teachers, but they will listen to their Coach!"
➤ This lesson will focus on the calling that we have as coaches for the kingdom of God to reach the generations of tomorrow.
CROSS REFERENCE: John 5: 17

WEEK 9—CHECK YOUR OIL—MATTHEW 7:1-5
"Character and Motives...Making wise choices in difficult situations"
➤ This lesson we will discuss the type of character and motivation God would like Christian-coaches to possess. We will also discuss the implications of character and motivation on a coach's ability to make Godly choices and decisions.
CROSS REFERENCE: I Corinthians 10:13

WEEK 10—MISSION POSSIBLE!—PROVERBS 19:21
"God's Purposes vs. Our Plans"
➤ During this lesson we will discuss what God's purpose was in creating coaches and athletes. We will also learn how to align our plans with God's by utilizing the "Double Win" philosophy.
CROSS REFERENCE: Philippians 2:13

WEEK 11—HE IS CALLING YOU OUT!—PHILIPPIANS 2:12-18
"Will you be a coach God can use-Any way He wants?"
➤ This purpose of this lesson is to show the importance of being obedient to God, in regard to the calling we have as both a Christian and a coach. We will also discuss how one Coach can impact the world!
CROSS REFERENCE: John 10:3-5

WEEK 12—GET IN THE GAME!—ISAIAH 49:6
"More is Caught than is Taught!"
➤ The purpose of this lesson is to give the Christian-coach practical and useful ways to leave a legacy for the kingdom of God in regard to mentoring players, leading staff bible studies, and servant leadership activities on the campus and in their communities.
CROSS REFERENCE: Matthew 28:19-20

WEEK 1

WHAT'S IN YOUR BOX?

*"What is the No. 1, central motivating
factor in your life?"*

READ: Colossians 3:23-25 (What does this mean to you?)

I. WHAT IS DRIVING YOU?

In his book Half-Time, Bob Buford is a CEO trying to decide what to do with
the second half of his life. To help him discern what to do, he hires a strategic
planning consultant that asks him to write down the No. 1 priority or central
motivating factor in his life from which all his secondary loyalties derive their
meaning or place of importance in his life. He then told him to put it in a box
that was placed on the table. Lastly, he informed the CEO that this one loyalty
will be the foundation of his life and it will affect all other areas of his
life…good or bad.

**What is (not what you wish it was) the No. 1, central motivating
factor or loyalty in your life?**

 EXTRA POINT: If you are having trouble narrowing your loyalties
down to one, remember that Jesus tells us that no one can serve two
masters, for if he/she does, they will hate the one and love the other.
(see Matthew 6:24) Find a way to get it down to one.

II. THE FILTER

The water filter in your refrigerator is designed to catch and keep all the impurities out of your drinking water. Like it or not, the No. 1 loyalty that you listed above is your filter for life. If the loyalty you listed was finances, then all the decisions you will make in your life will be based upon how those decisions will help you (directly or indirectly) save or make money. If your loyalty was your family, than all your major decisions will be based on how it affects your family and so on. Wouldn't you want a filter that protects you and keeps you safe, while still providing the nutrients you need? Jesus wants to be the filter that protects you from harm and directs your life.

What do you use as your filter when making decisions?
As a coach have you considered letting a relationship with Jesus be the No. 1 central motivating factor in your life? What would that look like?

Read aloud Jeremiah 29:11-13, How does this verse apply to you?

III. "HEY COACH! THIS IS THE 1ST DAY OF THE REST OF YOUR LIFE!"

God has given us all the power to choose what we want to put in our box! You have the power to choose to put Jesus Christ as the only thing in your box so He can be the foundation that will affect all areas of your life!

HOW TO TAKE ACTION:
1) What do I want to be remembered for?
2) What kind of Legacy do I want to leave behind?
3) Do I have a Destiny to fulfill?

*If you don't like what is in your box and want to put Jesus first in your life, or you do not have a personal relationship with Jesus Christ, please pray this short prayer and tell someone you did. "Lord Jesus, I need you! I want you to be the #1 loyalty in my life. Thank you for dying on the cross for me. Forgive me and cleanse me from my sins. I trust you as my Lord and Savior. Help me to be the person you created me to be. In Jesus' name. Amen.

MEMORIZE: Matthew 6:33

But seek first his kingdom and his righteousness, and all these things will be given to you as well.

ARE YOU F.A.T.?

*"Who we are, where we are going, and
how we are going to get there?*

READ: John 14:1-7

I. WHO IS JESUS TO YOU?

Whenever I took over a program at a school as the new head coach, my first
order of business with my team was to inform them of my expectations.
This began by informing the players of what it meant to be a player on our
team, what the goals are for the program, and how we are going to achieve
those goals. Before we talk about becoming a Legacy Builder for God's
kingdom we must decide who Jesus is and what it means to be a "Christian"
or a follower of Jesus Christ.

In the passage above, John the apostle writes to prove that Jesus is the Son
of God and that all who believe in Him will have eternal life. In Josh
McDowell's book, More Than a Carpenter, the author suggests that Jesus
could only be one of three things; 1) A Liar 2) A Lunatic   3) The Lord.

Look at the descriptions of each category and ask yourself who Jesus is to
you and why?

Liar: When Jesus claimed to be the Son of God, he knew that he was not
God; therefore he was lying and deliberately deceiving his followers. If he

was a liar, he was also a hypocrite because he told others to be honest no matter what the cost, while he himself lived a huge lie.

Lunatic: If it isn't possible for Jesus to be a liar, maybe he just thought he was God and was mistaken. If he was a lunatic, he was a crazy man and his teachings would have no depth and would not be mentally sound.

The Lord: He is actually who he says he is; the Lord of Lords and the King of Kings, the Son of God and the Savior who came to set us all free from our sins! (Read John 20:30-31)

If you believe that Jesus is Lord, then you must ask yourself...are my beliefs matching up with my behavior both as a coach and as a person? Why or why not?

II. WHAT IT MEANS TO BE A CHRISTIAN

As a Christian (or Christ follower), we inherit specific promises. We know that we are Accepted by God and a member of His team forever. We can also take comfort that we are Secure in Christ, meaning we are free forever from the condemnation of sin. And finally, we are assured that we are Significant as a child of God. He created each of us with specialized gifts and abilities to help further His kingdom! God sees you as His MVP!

III. ARE YOU F.A.T.?

If we hope to leave a Legacy for the kingdom of God as a coach, we must be F.A.T.! God is looking for individuals that are Faithful (fully trust in God), Available (willing to make time for God), Teachable (a coachable spirit and hunger to learn more about God). Are you F.A.T.?

MEMORIZE: John 3:16-17

For God so loved the world that he gave his one and only Son, that whoever believes in him shall not perish but have eternal life. For God did not send his Son into the world to condemn the world, but to save the world through him.

WEEK 3

GET WIRED!

*"Are you a Christian-coach or a
Coach that is a Christian?"*

READ: John 15:5

I. THE SOUL (READ JOB CHAPTER 42)

You can tell what is recorded on a man's soul by the way he reacts to
_____. Even though Job was under great adversity and was shocked by
comments from friends and family, he never responded in a negative fashion.

When your integrity has been questioned, how have you responded?

Are you a Christian-coach or a Coach that is a Christian? What is the
difference?

II. THE BODY

Our body _____ says a great deal about how we respond to difficult
situations. Throughout scripture many of God's leaders/coaches chose to
walk-away or not react to volatile situations in a worldly way even though
others were urging them to respond. WWJD? or HWJC? (How Would Jesus
Coach?)

Do you think before you act?

How do you think Jesus would coach?

What kind of messages do you send with your body or non-verbal language?

EXTRA POINT: "You may be the only Bible your players ever read!"

III. THE SPIRIT

The Spirit of God knows the true _____ of a person's heart. God will use tough situations to draw your intentions out.

HOW TO TAKE ACTION: The Word of God is the "Mechanism" that allows God speak to you on how to handle tough situations. The next time you find yourself in a difficult situation remember Romans 8:28 "And we know that in all things God works for the good of those who love him, who have been called according to his purpose." Then ask yourself...what would Jesus do? And do it!

MEMORIZE: Romans 8:28

And we know that in all things God works for the good of those who love him, who have been called according to his purpose.

Answer Key: 1. ADVERSITY 2. LANGUAGE 3. INTENTIONS

WEEK 4

THE TRAITS OF A LEGACY BUILDER

"What it takes to be the 'Real Deal'!"

READ: Titus 3:1-2

I. THE COACH/PERSON

As a coach, we always preach that there is no 'I' in TEAM. Just as a coach looks for _____ players, God looks for us to be _____ leaders on his team.

Leaders lead the way by going first, by going further and by giving maximal _____. Jesus Christ was the perfect 'servant leader'.

Are you the most important person on your team/family or are your players?

How do you model Servant Leadership to your team/family?
(Examples: Picking up equipment, getting the water for your players, doing the dishes or a chore that is not normally your responsibility, etc...)

II. THE EQUIPMENT

Just as a player must be equipped properly to be safe and perform optimally, God has equipped us, his servants with all the 'state of the art' equipment necessary to be great servant leaders in today's coaching world. He has given us a playbook called the _____. He has given us a Mentor in _____, and finally, he has given us players that we can _____ and _____ how to be great leaders themselves one day.

What is your most valuable piece of equipment and Why?

III. THE CHALLENGE

The challenge God puts before us is to set aside our selfish needs and _____ him. In order to do this as coaches we must _____ God, not try to _____ Him. We must be obedient to God and properly utilize the equipment he has entrusted to us.

HOW TO TAKE ACTION: Instead of being a dictator be a facilitator. When defining your goals focus on long term instead of short term. Treat and coach every player as if they were your child. Envision what you want your child/player to be like 30 years from now. Next, envision what type of legacy you want your players to leave the players of the future, and finally envision what you will say when God asks you how you did with his players/children.

MEMORIZE: Mark 10: 43-45
___

Not so with you. Instead, whoever wants to become great among you must be your servant, and whoever wants to be first must be slave of all. For even the Son of Man did not come to be served, but to serve, and to give his life as a ransom for many."

Answer Key: 1. UNSELFISH 2. SERVANT 3. SACRIFICE 4. BIBLE
5. JESUS CHRIST 6. DISCIPLE 7. TEACH 8. SERVE 9. TRUST 10. CONTROL

WEEK 5

COMMITMENT TO EXCELLENCE

"What are my goals and how do I reach them?"

READ: Matthew 6:19-25

I. THE PURSUIT OF EXCELLENCE (WORLDLY VS. GODLY)

Coaches and players set goals, such as a win every game, win a state championship and or win the national championship. We are in awe of championship rings and news clippings. We coach for a better job, more responsibility, more money, more wins! But God tells us He wants us to focus on _____ goals. Goals that can't be _____, rust or fade away. He wants us to coach to His glory and store up _____ in heaven. He wants us to coach for an _____ significance.

MAKE TWO LISTS: Worldly personal Goals & Godly personal Goals *(Examples: Win a state/national Championship **and** Align my plans with God's purpose)*

Write what you think God's list of goals would look like for you:

God's List of Goals '4' Me
1)
2)
3)
4)

II. YOUR TRAINING REGIMEN

Just as we tell our players that if they want to reach their maximum potential they must train every day without exception, we too, as coaches must train everyday in the Word and Prayer, if we are to reach our 'potential' as Godly coaches. You have seen the results of an athlete that trains religiously every day, why not let God train you for 30-60 minutes a day so you can maximize your potential!

Do you block out time to train with God on a daily basis?

Are you coachable-meaning, do you have a great attitude and give great effort in spending time with God?

A great coach knows a player can only control two things . . . their attitude and effort.

HOW TO TAKE ACTION: Make time for God. Schedule daily appointments with God for devotions and prayer in your day-timer or PDA. Write them in! Make sure you are visiting with God in a location where you will not be distracted and be sure that you are meeting with him at a time of the day when you are refreshed and ready to meet him.

MEMORIZE: I Corinthians 10:31

So whether you eat or drink or whatever you do, do it all for the glory of God.

Answer Key: 1. GODLY 2. STOLEN 3. TREASURES 4. ETERNAL

FEEDING THE MONSTER

"Is the job eating you up...reset your priorities?"

READ: Matthew 25: 14-30

I. TALENTS AND GIFTS

At some point in your life someone told you that you have a talent for coaching and or a gift for reaching young people. Those statements most likely helped propel you into the coaching profession.

Think back and please write (below) why you got into coaching?

Have your reasons for coaching changed? If yes, please state how.

II. TIME - (COACHES CREED: "LEAVE NO STONE UNTURNED...")

There are ___ hours in a day, ___ hours in a week and _____ hours in a year.

Your _____ determine how you utilize the time God has given you.

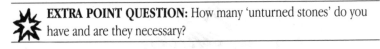

EXTRA POINT QUESTION: How many 'unturned stones' do you have and are they necessary?

Please list your priorities in order of importance?

This is how God would like your priorities to look...How does your list match-up?
1. Your Personal Relationship with Jesus Christ (Faith)
2. Your Family
3. Your Players
4. Your Job

III. BALANCE

God can do more in 6 minutes than a person can do in 6 months. God is the ultimate _____ and has perfect _____. If we hope to achieve balance in our lives we must have our _____ in the proper order and God will honor our _____. If we are not right with God and close to him he cannot guide us, and if He cannot guide us we will be at the mercy of a chaotic world.

HOW TO TAKE ACTION: Look at your priorities above and try to narrow them to four. Next, across from each priority list the number of hours per week you put towards each one. Pray to God on a daily basis to help you utilize your time wisely for the kingdom of God and to keep your priorities in order. (If you are a Head Coach, ask your assistants to list their priorities and time commitments and see if you, as a Head Coach, are allowing them to be productive people in God's kingdom.)

MEMORIZE: Matthew 6: 33-34

But seek first his kingdom and his righteousness, and all these things will be given to you as well. Therefore do not worry about tomorrow, for tomorrow will worry about itself. Each day has enough trouble of its own.

Answer Key: 1. 24 2. 168 3. 8,736 4. PRIORITIES 5. PLANNER 6. TIMING
7. PRIORITIES 8. FAITHFULNESS

TAMING THE TONGUE

"Living a Coach's lifestyle...the way God wants!"

Read: James 3: 1-12

I. THE TALK

A person's _____ displays what type of _____ he or she has.

Do you build players/people up or tear them down?
What does it mean to 'speak greatness' into someone?

⭐ **EXTRA POINT:** "A good coach tells a player what he can do, not what he can't do." Fisher DeBerry

---

II. THE POWER OF THE 'PUT-UP' (A SINCERE, SPECIFIC COMPLIMENT) GAME

'Put-Ups' keep us _____ positive and hopeful. 'Put-Ups' keep us free from the negative power of _____ shifts.

(Example: "Son that is the best decision I have seen a player make since I have been the coach here. You have come a long way and you are going to be a great player here!")

Describe a situation when someone said something negative to you that you have never forgotten. What type of an impact did it have on you?

Describe a situation when someone spoke greatness into you. What type of impact did it have on you?

III. THE WALK/THE BATTLE (READ EPHESIANS 6: 10-20)

Your daily walk as a Christian-coach in today's world is a _____.
Satan does not want you to succeed as a Christian-coach. You are in a
_____ and your _____ speak louder than your _____!

How would your players describe you?

How would your greatest adversary describe you? Do you like their perception? If not how can you change it?

HOW TO Tame the Tongue and Walk the Walk:
Have a clean heart. Ask God to renew your heart and to guard what you say everyday. THINK before you speak. Is what you are going to say True, Helpful, Inspiring, Necessary and Kind? Next, surround yourself with Godly people, if none are available, ask God to send someone into your life.

Finally...be slow to speak...and quick to listen!

MEMORIZE: Proverbs 29: 20

Do you see a man who speaks in haste? There is more hope for a fool than for him.

Answer Key: 1. TONGUE 2. CHARACTER 3. MENTALLY 4. MOMENTUM 5. BATTLE 6. FIGHT 7. ACTIONS 8. WORDS

SEED PLANTERS

*"Kids may not listen to parents or teachers,
but they will listen to their Coach!"*

READ: Proverbs 22:6

I. YOUR CALLING

In a world where quick results and fast food are the norm, the Christian-coach is called to do _____ than just win games. We are called to _____ seeds of hope in the _____ of tomorrow. We are called by God to share our _____ through words and actions with our players, with a hope that someday the seed will take hold, develop strong roots, grow and give them _____ life.

Is coaching an occupation (job) or a vocation (calling)? Why?

II. THE FIELD

Just as a farmer must till the soil before he/she can plant the seeds, a Christian-coach must get his/her players ready for life. _____ is the only profession that allows for so many opportunities to teach and mold the leaders of tomorrow. What a great _____ and _____.

What does your harvest field look like?

(Example: A large field of corn that needs constant care and is growing at a rapid pace...)

III. THE HARVEST (READ MATTHEW 9:37-38)

If a planted seed isn't _____ and fed by the farmer and nature it will _____. As coaches, it is not enough to just plant the seed. We must continue to care for our players on a daily basis. And just as the farmer trusts God to bring rain, we too must _____ God to work in the _____ of our players as we pray for them.

How much care do you take in the seeds (players) you sow?

Are you praying for God to help your players grow?

HOW TO TAKE ACTION: Ask God for courage to share your faith, and pray for your players daily. Especially pray for the ones with which you are having problems. Look for teachable moments and don't give up. Remember, some seeds take longer to sprout than others.

MEMORIZE: John 5:17

Jesus said to them, "My Father is always at his work to this very day, and I, too, am working."

Answer Key: 1. MORE 2. PLANT 3. PARENTS 4. FAITH 5. ETERNAL
6. COACHING 7. CALLING 8. RESPONSIBILITY 9. NURTURED
10. DIE 11. TRUST 12. HEARTS

CHECK YOUR OIL!

"Character & Motives...Making wise choices during difficult situations"

READ: Matthew 7:1-5

I. THE OIL (CHARACTER)

Coaches in the South have a saying when it comes to measuring a player's character; they call it 'checking his oil'. As coaches, we often question our players' and colleague's character at the drop of a hat; however, Christ tells us to look at our own _____ before pointing the finger at others.

How would coaches in your league describe your character?
How would the parents of your players describe your character?
Do you like their perception? If not, how can you change it?

II. THE FUEL (MOTIVES)

If the fuel in a vehicle is not _____ and _____, the engine will not respond properly and will eventually sustain damage. Our hearts are not much different. If our motives are not _____ and _____ when making decisions, we too will eventually sustain damage to our lives and possibly to those around us.

Think of a time when you had to make a difficult coaching decision-what were the motivating factors that lead you to your decision?(i.e., winning etc.) Did you consult your Father in Heaven? If so, why?

III. POOR DECISIONS + TEMPTATION = WEAKENED CHARACTER

Many coaches think they lose a game based upon one bad decision, but most of us know that usually it is a series of small mistakes that slowly causes defeat. Satan is no different; he looks to attack our _____ spots and _____ areas first, in hopes of slowly weakening our character until it cracks. As Christian-coaches we must protect ourselves by utilizing _____ wisdom and by maintaining _____ and Godly motives when making decisions.

What are some of the ways you can protect yourself from making poor decisions? *(Examples:No snap decisions, have an accountability partner, being in the Word...)*

HOW TO TAKE ACTION: The next time you are tempted or in a difficult situation think of, I Corinthians 10:13, and remember God will not permit you to be tempted more than you can stand and when you are tempted, pray and He will give you a way out so that you will be able to make a good decision.

MEMORIZE: I Corinthians 10:13

No temptation has seized you except what is common to man. And God is faithful; he will not let you be tempted beyond what you can bear. But when you are tempted, he will also provide a way out so that you can stand up under it.

Answer Key: 1. FLAWS 2. PURE 3. CLEAN 4. PURE 5. CLEAN 6. BLIND 7. VULNERABLE 8. GOD'S 9. PURE

MISSION POSSIBLE!

"God's Purposes vs. Our Plans"

READ: Proverbs 19:21

I. SCRIPTING FOR SUCCESS

As coaches we spend countless hours preparing game plans, practice plans, and even contingency plans. But sometimes even our best plans fail. As the Master Coach, _____ has written a flawless game plan that has a specific purpose for each one of us. It is our calling as coaches to see what His _____ is for us and align our _____ with His purpose.

What do you think God's purpose is in having you as a coach on His team? *(Example: He wants me to be his point guard and lead other coaches/players to Christ)*

II. GOD'S PLAN FOR COACHES AND ATHLETES

Have you ever wondered why God created Coaches and Athletes? Ask a few of your athletes and colleagues for their thoughts and write their responses below.

READ: I Corinthians 9:22-23

Athletics is a microcosm of life. It mirrors life's situations in the arena and on the field. Sport gives us opportunities to display how God wants us to handle success and failure. As Christian-coaches, we believe God created athletes and coaches to demonstrate great _____ and to _____ the weak.

III. FOLLOWING GOD'S GAME PLAN (I CORINTHIANS 9:24-27)

As Christian-coaches, God wants us to maintain a 'Double Win' philosophy. In other words, God demands that we teach all our athletes how to_____ _____ and strive for the _____ that is set before them. We should strive to have our athletes win in the athletic arena and in _____, specifically _____ life.

 EXTRA POINT: Consider writing a mission statement for yourself, as a coach in God's kingdom.

HOW TO MAKE SURE YOUR PLANS ALIGN WITH GOD'S PURPOSE for YOU: The next time you are not sure if you are doing what God wants you to do:
1) Be still, pray and ask God for clarification. (Fasting, keep your antenna up!)
2) Read the Bible.
3) Seek Counsel from other Godly people (perhaps outside the situation)
4) Proceed and look for affirmations from the Holy Spirit in people, the Bible and circumstances.
NOTE: Remember, if it is not of God it is not from God.

MEMORIZE: I John 2:17

"The World and its desires pass away, but the man who does the will of God lives forever."

Answer Key: 1. GOD 2. PURPOSE 3. PLANS 4. CHARACTER 5. CHAMPION 6. WORK HARD 7. PRIZE 8. LIFE 9. ETERNAL

HE'S CALLING YOU OUT!

"Will you be a Coach God can use — Any way He wants?"

READ: Philippians 2:12-18

I. ORDINARY PEOPLE EXTRAORDINARY THINGS!

More games have been won through the efforts of _____ coaches than all the famous coaches combined. More people have come to Christ through the efforts of _____ people than all the famous evangelists combined!

Ask yourself; will I be a coach God can use?
Will I be an obedient team player and let Him use me any way He wants?
What do these questions mean to you? What keeps us from being obedient?

II. IT ONLY TAKES ONE!

How many times have you told one of your players that if they would just step out and raise their level of play it would _____ all the other players around them? We see it everyday in the athletics, one person with a _____ and a purpose takes their game to a higher level and their _____ inspires their teammates to do the same and consequently, together everyone achieves more (i.e. Michael Jordan).

God wants to use you to inspire others for his kingdom, what are some ways you can be useful to God in your coaching? *(Example: Living out your faith through coaching, actions speak louder than words...)*

III. IMPACTING THE INFRA-STRUCTURE OR INNER WORKINGS OF THE COACHING CULTURE

An apple _____ from the inside out and usually by the time you notice, it is too late. Players, coaches and teams are not any different. That is why God has _____ you to 'impact the infrastructure', by giving your players the love and knowledge of _____ that they need to be solid individuals in the game of life.

What happened to Jonah when he didn't go to Nineveh? (If you don't know the story read Jonah Chapter 1: 1-17)

 EXTRA POINT: "It only takes one coach who is obedient to his/her calling to inspire others. If you are obedient it frees God to do great things!"

HOW TO 'IMPACT THE INFRA-STRUCTURE': Sell out to putting the kingdom of God first and winning second. Winning is a by-product of aiming for perfection in Jesus Christ. Realize that God uses ordinary people to do extraordinary things. He wants to use you, just let him!

MEMORIZE: Colossians 3:23-24

Whatever you do, work at it with all your heart, as working for the Lord, not for men, since you know that you will receive an inheritance from the Lord as a reward. It is the Lord Christ you are serving.

Answer Key: 1. ORDINARY 2. ORDINARY 3. INSPIRE 4. VISION
5. PASSION 6. ROTS 7. CALLED 8. JESUS CHRIST

GET IN THE GAME!

"More is Caught than is Taught!"

READ: Isaiah 49:6 Is this Scripture calling you out!

I. CLINIC TALK

Have you ever been to a coaching clinic and the information you received from the speakers was just fabulous; but as you returned to your team and began to implement the concepts into your practices, it just wasn't as easy as it sounded? In other words, you loved the concept and what it could do for you, but you needed more specific details and instructions to make it fit into your style.

That is the purpose of this lesson—

To begin, just jot down any questions you may want to bring up for discussion.

II. IMPACTING PLAYERS/TEAM — "CREATE MEMORABLE EXPERIENCES"

You can impact your players and your team on a surface level with a change in philosophy through speeches and signs, but you can change your player's lives forever by letting them experience being a servant-leader first hand and by you and your staff creating memorable experiences. Always look for teachable moments!

Examples: Waiter/Waitress Day in the cafeteria, Drink servers at fast food restaurants, pump gas at local gas stations, operation blessing to other teams, 12 ways to bless your opponent, and lastly a "quality use of a waste of time" — just being together as a team, grilling out or meeting as an FCA huddle or just a team night that is not related to your sport.

III. GO DEEPER WITH PLAYERS/COACHES -MENTOR SOMEONE — "MORE IS CAUGHT THAN IS TAUGHT"

Christ chose 12 and went even deeper with 3 of the 12. If we are to further the kingdom of God we must do it the same way Christ did...multiplication... one person at a time.

Examples: Ask God to rise up one or two individuals that you can mentor for a semester. It can be a player and or another coach. Agree to set some guidelines for accountability and commitment, but more importantly just spend time together once a week teaching and learning about what it means to have a personal relationship with Jesus Christ.

IV. GET IN THE GAME! — GET INVOLVED!

You will never know until you've tried. You have the time just keep your priorities in order..but remember God's kingdom comes first.

Examples: Lead an FCA huddle on your campus, start a Legacy Builder study with coaches at your school or in your community, start an accountability group with fellow coaches, see where God is working and join him! check out www.coachesministry.com and start "Winning God's Way" bible study (www.crosstrainingpublishing.com).

MEMORIZE: Matthew 28:19-20

Therefore go and make disciples of all nations, baptizing them in the name of the Father and of the Son and of the Holy Spirit, and teaching them to obey everything I have commanded you. And surely I am with you always, to the very end of the age."

STUDY LEADER'S GUIDE

DEAR LEGACY BUILDER LEADER,

Thank you for being obedient to your calling and welcome to the awesome and vital task of helping men and women in the most difficult profession in the world (coaching) see how God can use them to further His kingdom and leave a legacy. By accepting this call and challenge, you align yourself with the many followers of Jesus Christ who have listened to his call and agreed to commit to further His kingdom. As a Legacy Builder study leader, you may never completely know the impact you have for the kingdom until we all get to Heaven and are with the Father, but at that time it will be clear to all!

So I encourage you to be faithful with a little and to be patient with yourself and your group. It is not up to you to change people's hearts...that is God's job. It is your job to share the word of God and the biblical principles included in this study and God will do the rest. Remember, the Word of God never comes back void!

May you enjoy the weeks ahead, and may you enjoy God's blessing and favor as you serve Him faithfully with your study group. One of the greatest things Jesus did was to help people see how God can use them to further His kingdom in the everyday work of their lives. My prayer is that you too, will be blessed with Christ's presence and power as you strive to help others see the impact they can have, not only for their own eternity, but the eternity of their families, players and colleagues!

WHY A LEGACY BUILDER STUDY?

The Legacy Builder study series came from God and was developed to fulfill a need for coaches to have a relevant Bible study. I wrote the Legacy Builder series to have curriculum for our area coaches' bible studies for the Fellowship of Christian Athletes Coaches Ministry in Colorado. Several years ago, God brought a man into my life named Scotty Kessler. As a head football coach at the collegiate level, I brought Scotty in as a consultant to assess our football program and coaching staff. Through those meetings God used Scotty to teach me how to integrate Biblical principles into my coaching philosophy and program. My life was changed forever, as I finally had been given the knowledge and tools I needed for God to use me to minister to coaches and athletes through my coaching. As I went deeper in my relationship with God, I found myself being called to the ministry with the yearning to tell others how coaching with Biblical principles changed my life! However, one of my biggest struggles as a Christian coach, was finding Bible studies that were relevant to my career as a coach. Surely, Jesus had something to say to a person that worked for a nickel an hour, 80 to 90 hours a week, was paid to win, and had hundreds of people that would listen to him. And besides, I needed to know what Jesus had to say about handling an angry parent or getting fired! Needless to say, I didn't find any studies in the book stores that dealt with those topics. After visiting with Johnny Square (chaplain for the Colorado State University football program) I decided to ask God to help me put on paper just a few of the principles I have been taught and that have allowed me to become close enough to God so that he may use me to leave a legacy for His kingdom through coaching.

YOUR LEGACY BUILDER GROUP

You are going to find an eager group of coaches in your weekly meetings. You are going to find that this study crosses all gender, race and sport. Coaches from all different levels and sports are going to enjoy great prayer time and fellowship while they learn. Every person wants to know how they can improve and every Christian coach wants to know how they can be a Christian and still strive to win and compete to God's glory! You are going to have a ball!

If you are a first time group leader or inexperienced group leader, you will enjoy the leadership guide and short lessons. Everything is based on the word of God and each lesson begins and ends with scripture. As Paul said, "My speech and my preaching not with persuasive words of human wisdom, but in demonstration of the Spirit and of power, that your faith should not be in the wisdom of men but in the power of God" (1 Corinthians 2: 4-5).

All you have to bring to the table each week is a willingness to serve God and others, the truth of God's word, and a total dependence upon God to do His work.

As you pray each week for those things and God's guidance, you will hear coaches share stories about what they have learned and how God is working in their lives. You will see lives transformed and you too will grow closer to God. Finally, as you finish the study with your group you will see the power of God move as your group members want to start their own Legacy Builder study groups with other coaches. And that is what leaving a legacy is all about! Praise God.

GROUND RULES FOR YOUR SMALL GROUP

To ensure that everyone in your group is on the same page, I would encourage you to lead the group in making 3 commitments:

1) Everyone agrees to and completes the Legacy Builder group covenant sheet located at the beginning of the study booklet. You don't need to collect the sheets but everyone should fill one out for their own level of commitment.
2) Everyone commits to spending time prior to meeting in preparation for the lesson. This is not a difficult task as the lessons are short and the answers are located in the back of the booklet.
3) Everyone commits to ask God to change their lives according to the Biblical truths presented.

THE STRUCTURE OF EACH LEGACY BUILDER LESSON

Each week, God leads coaches through a dynamic, life changing process through the lessons. Each lesson begins with a topic and scripture that ties to that specific topic or principle. There are fill in the blanks along with questions to facilitate thought and discussion. Finally, the lesson concludes with a "How to take Action" section which gives the coach practical tools and steps for how to implement the principle taught that day into their daily routines. But most importantly, each lesson concludes with scripture that is again relevant to the lesson's topic and the student is expected to memorize the verse or verses. Memorization is a key part of the weekly lesson as the Word of God is the sword of the Spirit.

DISCUSSION LEADER'S GUIDE

HOW TO START A LEGACY BUILDER GROUP:

Get copies of the Legacy Builder study and show a copy to the coaches you would like to meet with. Ask them to glance at the study and see if they would be interested in spending time together in fellowship and learning as coaches. This can be coaches from any sport or any level and can be a male or female. The only criteria you may want to stand firm on is that they are a coach or have been a coach. The optimum sized group would be eight to twelve assuming that some coaches may have to miss occasionally. Decide that you will meet for 11 weeks at a consistent time and location, preferably a room in a church that is a private setting. We have found that 6am is a great time for coaches to meet, though it is early, there are minimal conflicts. If the group gels, you can continue to meet and move to the 2nd study in the Legacy Builder Series Part 2— "The Quest" which is also an 12 week series.

WEEK 1:

Have coffee and soft drinks available if possible. Set up the room so that you are all sitting in a circle or at least around a table. It is important that everyone can have eye contact. If you are meeting over lunch, allow fifteen minutes to eat and then begin the meeting. Distribute a copy of the Legacy Builder study booklet to each member. Go over the twelve week schedule in regard to start time/finish time and meeting place. I would also encourage you send a sign up sheet around with email and phone number information in case a meeting must be cancelled or postponed due to inclimate weather. Briefly discuss the Legacy Builder Group Covenant in the beginning of the booklet and encourage them to fill it out and keep it in their books. Next, tell them that each meeting will begin with you asking them to share what is going on in their lives and how the group can pray for them. Every meeting will begin with fellowship, sharing and prayer. This is vital and cannot be missed. Assign the first lesson as next week's assignment and ask them to be prepared to share if necessary. Next, go around and ask each person what school they are from and what sport(s) they coach and also have them share vitals about their family. This is a great way to break the ice and get to know each other on a more personal level. Be sure to point out that we are here to support and encourage one another and not convict each other. Lastly, close with a prayer and always start and adjourn on time! Many times, coaches must leave early to get to school on time, just make sure they understand that is fine and any information they may have missed they can get from a colleague or yourself.

TYPICAL WEEK:

Each week begin with each person sharing what is happening in their lives and any prayer requests they might have, you are to go last. As the facilitator, you are going to be the one praying following the requests so I would encourage you to have a spiral notebook that you write the person's name and prayer request in for each meeting. This will allow for two things: One, you will be able to keep track of the requests and petition all of them to God that day, and two, you will have a log at the end of eleven weeks of everyone's prayer requests and if you like at the end you can separate each person's prayers and share with them how God answered their prayers and others.

- Fellowship/Sharing & Prayer requests   20 Minutes
- Weekly Legacy Builder Lesson   30 Minutes
- Closing Group Prayer   10 Minutes

ALTERNATIVE TO TYPICAL WEEK:

Prepare to let the fellowship/sharing and prayer time go where God wants it to one meeting. Or if something has happened in the media that is of merit for discussion in regard to the coaching profession prepare a 20 minute discussion and facilitate it, finishing with prayer.

I would encourage you to wait at least 4-5 weeks into the lessons before doing this, so you have more of a biblical base for the discussions. Also, I would not do this more than once as the series is twelve weeks long and you don't want the weeks to get too long.

LEADING A LESSON/DISCUSSION:

The key to a successful meeting and group discussion is your ability as the leader, to insure that you keep a delicate balance between each group member having the opportunity for input and making sure the material in the lesson is covered adequately for learning to occur. Your role is to keep the meeting moving while encouraging each coach to render his/her thoughts on the subject that day. If questions come up that are off the subject, simply suggest that we discuss that at another time. If someone tends to dominate the dialogue (including you) privately, ask them to help you draw out the more introverted members of the group. If you have a shy member, tread lightly, but ask them every so often, "_____, what do you think about this question?"

You don't have to be a graduate of a seminary or an experienced Bible teacher to facilitate and lead the Legacy Builder Study Series. If someone asks you a question that you don't feel you can answer, just be honest and say you will try to find the answer, but you do not know, and move on.

Finally, the Legacy Builder Study Series is written in such a format that I would encourage you to share your own stories or experiences in regard to the topic of each lesson.

Not only will this make you more comfortable but it will facilitate thoughts in those around you and they will begin to share.

FINAL THOUGHTS:

As the weeks go by, I would encourage you each week to send a sign in sheet around in case phone numbers change and to keep track of individuals for your own purposes. It is not for attendance purposes. Also, the Legacy Builder study is written so that if someone does wish to attend after the meetings have started they may do so. It is not optimal but you don't want to limit God from working!

You will be richly blessed as you cover your group in prayer and see God working...thank you for helping further the kingdom!

B R I E F N O T E S F O R L E A D E R S
O N W E E K L Y L E S S O N S

WEEK 1 - WHAT'S IN YOUR BOX?

➤ Have a cardboard box and note cards for people to write down their No. 1 Central motivating factor in their life. Now ask them to place it in the box and read them aloud without using names.

WEEK 2 - ARE YOU F.A.T.?

➤ Make sure you have a Legacy Builder bookmark for each book. This will allow you to remind each other about who you are in Christ.

WEEK 3 - GET WIRED

"Are you a Christian-coach or a coach that is a Christian?"
The purpose of this lesson is to assess where you are as a coach both in and out of the athletic arena.

START: Have someone read John 15:5

Tips:
➤ *Dwell on the question:* Are you a Christian-coach or a coach that is a Christian? The difference being that a coach that is a Christian thinks that when he/she steps on the court or field they can do and act however they want. This same person may not intentionally sin, but the heat of the battle causes them to do things they wish they hadn't and they apologize to God and everyone later. Conversely, a Christian-Coach sees things through Christ's eyes and is thinking like Christ and thinks before he or she acts. They see everything with an eternal significance.
➤ Talk about the fact that sometimes our body language, like turning our back on a player or rolling our eyes speaks volumes.
➤ *Highlight Extra Point:* "You may be the only Bible your players ever read!"

How to Take Action:
➤ Romans 8:28 is a mechanism to get the coach to stop, slow down and think before he or she acts. The scripture allows the Holy Spirit to speak to you and see things through Christ's eyes first as a Christian-coach. Read Memory Verse.

WEEK 4 — THE TRAITS OF A LEGACY BUILDER

"What it takes to be the real deal"
This lesson will focus on being a servant leader, messenger and sent one. We will embrace the fact that in order to be the greatest, you must become the least.

START: Have someone read Titus 3:1-2

Tips:
➤ *Dwell on the question:* How do you model servant leadership to your players/family?
➤ Next move into what are the repercussions of them replicating your model. Can it help you win? Absolutely...we are only as strong as our weakest link right?
➤ You are also teaching the fact that no one is more important than anyone else. Humbleness—
➤ What about their families...are they being servants or being served? Men help your wives!!
➤ Move down to The Challenge segment. The hardest thing for coaches to do is not have control. Coaching is all about control. Control our players, the officials, the game outcome.

God doesn't want us to just sit around and do nothing, but He does want us to trust Him and let Him work.

How to Take Action:
➤ Ask the coaches what they want their own kids to turn out like when the kids are 35 and what are they doing now to help insure that happens.
➤ Ask the coaches what type of coach they want coaching their grand children because their players are the coaches of tomorrow! Read Memory Verse.

WEEK 5 — COMMITMENT TO EXCELLENCE

"What are my goals and how do I reach them?"
The purpose of this lesson is to discern Godly goals from worldly goals for a Christian coach, and to help the coach understand how to reach and measure those goals.

Start: Have someone read Matthew 6: 19-25

Tips:
➤ If you can, find some magazines or sports articles that glorify coaches and winning as the only thing that determines success in life. Show them to the group after you read the first paragraph of the lesson.
➤ Focus on the fact that it okay to have personal goals and to want to win, but God wants us to strive for goals that assure us eternal life and that further the kingdom.
➤ The 4 goals God wants for us in order are:
  1) An intimate Love relationship with Him
  2) Minister to your family
  3) Minister to your players
  4) Glorify God through your job
➤ You may want to ask the group why are the above Godly goals?
➤ When discussing their Training Regimen emphasize the importance of blocking out time with God and how important it is to be fresh. Morning time is the best, turn off the phone, and shut the door.
➤ Have people share different styles of quiet times and what works for others, but emphasize that all quiet time must involve the Word, prayer and watching and listening to God.

How to Take Action:
➤ Discuss the importance of spending time with God alone and how this will draw you closer to Him and you will then have the fuel you need to do His work. Read Memory Verse.

WEEK 6 - FEEDING THE MONSTER

"Is the Job eating you up...reset your priorities"
This lesson will focus on time management. We will discuss what a Christian-coach's priorities look like and how a coach can maintain balance within a hectic schedule.

Start: Have someone read Matthew 25:14-30, The parable of the talents was chosen because we want coaches to remember that God has given you many talents and gifts...the question: are you making the most of the gifts He has given you for the kingdom?

Tips:
➤ Have coaches share why they got into coaching. When discussing if reasons have changed, bring up the fact that many coaches are still coaching because they cannot afford to lose the stipend or they are so close to becoming the next head coach that they won't retire etc.
➤ Focus on the element of time and that all coaches wish a day was 36 hours and not 24.
➤ Discuss what unturned stones they have and are there any stones that could be left unturned or have someone else turn them over.
➤ State that coaches shift around priorities based upon the importance of them at the time, i.e., "I can't eat lunch today honey, the principal said a parent called and wants to talk to me." Not good, but a reality.
➤ Focus on the statement "How are you utilizing the time God has given you?"
➤ Emphasize that God can do more in 6 minutes that we can do in 6 months.
➤ *For added discussion:* What about the things coaches can't control...do they leave it up to God or do they worry and waste time on them? Why?

How to Take Action: Have coaches share their findings of listings their hours next to their priorities and discuss praying for God to help you utilize the time He has given us wisely. Read Memory Verse.

WEEK 7 — TAMING THE TONGUE

"Living a Coach's lifestyle...the way God wants"
The purpose of this lesson is to help the coach 'talk the talk and walk the walk' of a Christian-coach on a daily basis.

Start: Have someone read James 3: 1-12, This is a long passage but is filled with great nuggets of information for the coach, beginning with the fact that teachers are judged more strictly and that praising and cursing come out of the same mouth. We can tame wild animals, control a huge ship with a small rudder but we cannot control our tongues. You are going to teach them today a way to coach and talk that will change them and their players forever. Instead of always criticizing and telling people what they are doing wrong, you are going to tell them what they are doing right and because they are so good at what they are doing they will do other great things in the future!

Tips:
> ➤ Focus on building players up not tearing them down. The marine mentality works for a while but soon your players will quit or leave.
> ➤ When you speak greatness into someone, you speak a vision of greatness into his or her mind, i.e., "You are really improving, you are going to be the best shortstop to have ever played here."
> ➤ *The Put-up game:* During practice tell your players they have 10 minutes to give 3 other players on the team a sincere specific compliment, i.e., "Great hit Billy, you really drove that ball to right field well" or "Rick, I really appreciate how hard you work everyday even though you have not got to play much, thank you." It may sound hokey, but when people build each other up all the time it creates a climate of belief and positive attitudes that helps your team play better. Remember, happy players play better! You can also do the put ups following a practice or game with parents around to hear it. This has a huge impact on parents that don't see their children complaining, but instead lifting others up even after a loss!
> ➤ *Additional comment to share:* God is easy to please but hard to satisfy, we don't want blind obedience we want changed hearts in our players and coaches.

How to Take Action: Ask coaches to THINK before they speak but to also implement the "put up game" into their practices and games. Remember, don't compromise perfection but encourage your players! Read Memory Verse.

WEEK 8 — SEED PLANTERS

"Kids may not listen to their parents or teachers but they will listen to their coach!" This lesson will focus on the calling that we have as coaches for the kingdom of God to reach the generations of tomorrow.

Start: Have someone read Proverbs 22:6

Tips:
➤ Focus on the fact that we as coaches are called, it is not a job it is a ministry.
➤ Lastly focus on the fact that some people in God's kingdom are planters, waterers, harvesters. Some people are only one, some two, and others all three or two of three. Ask coaches to think where they fit in that model. Also remind them God can move them from category to category.
➤ Share what your harvest field looks like and ask other coaches to share what their fields look like.
➤ Share the importance and power of prayer and how God does the work if we pray.
➤ *Additional comment for college coaches:* Pray more and recruit less, ask God to send you the right recruits for your program. Have prayer be the primary supplement in the equation.

How to Take Action: Emphasize the fact that it may take some seeds longer to sprout than others. State how players sometimes come back years later thanking you for something you don't even remember saying or doing. Read Memory Verse.

WEEK 9 — CHECK YOUR OIL

"Character and Motives...making wise choices in difficult situations"
This lesson we will discuss the type of character and motivation God would like Christian-coaches to possess. We will also discuss the implications of character and motivation on a coach's ability to make Godly choices and decisions.

Start: Have someone read Matthew 7:1-5

Tips:
➤ Focus on question regarding the perception people have of you and how you can change that if you don't like it.
➤ Discuss the motivating factors that lead to decisions in the coaching world, i.e., win at all costs, keep your job, please parents, favorite player, don't like the other coach etc.
➤ Ask coaches if they go to the Father in Heaven for advice...First? If so, why do they or why should they?
➤ Spend the majority of the time talking about blind spots that we have and

where we are vulnerable. We are all taught when driving to compensate for the blind spots in our mirrors by doing additional things like looking over our shoulder and checking other mirrors to insure safety. As Christian-coaches we have blind spots and we need to know what they are and how we can protect ourselves. Ask the coaches to make a list of their blind spots and how they can pray and take steps to protect themselves from harm.

How to Take Action: Read Memory Verse. Finish by talking about temptation and how our God is sovereign and if we allow Him to help us through prayer He will show us a way out. Trust the Word!

Reemphasize the importance of their quiet time each day.

WEEK 10 — MISSION POSSIBLE

"God's Purposes vs. Our Plans"
During this lesson we will discuss what God's purpose was in creating coaches and athletes. We will also learn how to align our plans with God's by utilizing the "Double Win" philosophy.

Start: Have someone read Proverbs 19:21

Tips:
➤ Focus on the question regarding what they think God's purpose is in having you as a coach on His team.
➤ Ask why God created coaches and athletes and read aloud 1 Corinthians 9:22-23.
➤ Discuss the Double Win philosophy and ask them if they ever thought about what their overall philosophy is when coaching. Lead them into the extra point note and writing a personal mission statement as a coach and parent or spouse.

How to Take Action: Go through the steps for making sure your plans align with God's purpose for you. If you have knowledge of Fasting principles it may be a good time to give a hand out or share verbally. Read Memory Verse.

WEEK 11 — HE'S CALLING YOU OUT

"Will you be a coach God can use any way He wants?"
The purpose of this lesson is to show the importance of being obedient to God, in regard to the calling we have as both a Christian and a coach. We will also discuss how on Coach can impact the world!

Start: Have someone read Philippians 2: 12-18 and tell the coaches that this morning they are going to be pushed to the edge of the cliff or to the edge of the nest. By the end of the lesson they will have decided in their heart if they are going to utilize and pass on the knowledge they now possess (coaching and living with Biblical principles) and let God use them or not.

Tips:
➤ Focus on the question regarding what they think God's purpose is in having you as a coach on His team. Lead them into the fact that a coach's favorite player is the most unselfish, team guy, that will do whatever we ask them to do without question. Immediate obedience.
➤ Discuss some ways coaches can be useful to God i.e., language, speaking opportunities, when people ask you why you do things the way you do, using stories from the Bible to make points or motivate etc.
➤ In discussing what it means to impact the infrastructure, reinforce the purpose of the Legacy Builder series is to get them closer to God and pass on or leave a legacy for the kingdom of God.

How to Take Action: Reinforce the fact that God has raised this ministry and them for such a time as this! Emphasize the fact that God uses ordinary people to do ordinary things! Read Memory Verse.

WEEK 12 - GET IN THE GAME

"More is caught than is Taught!"
The purpose of this lesson is to give the Christian-coach practical and useful ways to leave a legacy for the kingdom of God in regard to mentoring players, leading staff Bible studies, and servant leadership activities on the campus and in their communities.

Start: Have someone read Isaiah 49:6 and talk about the question; is it too much for God to ask us to do something for Him? Quick answer...no.

Tips:
➤ Simply follow what is written and for each heading share your own thoughts or things you have done and then have others in the group share. The thrust of the lesson is to give them ideas and things they can do immediately to further God's kingdom and leave a legacy!

Finishing the Meeting:
➤ Finish by sending a sign up list around that includes the following:
➤ Who would like to do another Legacy Builder study next semester
➤ Who is going to start and lead a Legacy Builder study group in their school or community
➤ Who would like to purchase booklets for mentoring your athletes "Winning God's Way"
➤ Who is going to start a team bible study using "Winning God's Way"
➤ Who would like to become involved in a one on one mentoring program to go deeper

You will also have evaluations for them to fill out so you can better minister to their needs. Lastly, finish with a group prayer!

DESCRIPTION OF ACTIVITIES LISTED IN LESSON 10

"Create Memorable Experiences"
➤ Waiter/Waitress Day in Cafeteria (Have your players be greeters, waiters, busboys and servers in the school cafeteria. Brief them before hand that they are servant leaders and some people may not appreciate them, but don't worry about it and have fun with it. Then debrief them later as to how the experience as a servant felt and how people responded to their kindness and unselfishness. Also, discuss how the world does not understand why someone would help someone else for no apparent reason other than love.)
➤ Drink Servers at fast food restaurants (Call the restaurants ahead of time and tell what you are doing and make sure they understand they are not there to do work for the employees. Have your players stand by the drink machines and ask people if they can fill up their beverage for them. Again, brief your players before hand and tell them to accept no tips. When people are finished with their meal, have your players ask if they can take their trays to the garbage for them and etc...Again, debrief and tie in the discussion to how unselfishness and servant leadership can make the world and your team a better place.)

➤ Operation Blessings (This is an activity that is broad in scope. This is where you as the coach decide how you can bless people in positions of servant hood, such as bus drivers, janitors, maintenance people, waiters, waitresses, cooks and also other teams on campus. Bus trips and team meals are great opportunities to bless people. At any time you the coach can present a t-shirt, hat, certificate or game ball to the bus driver, maintenance guys, or restaurant personnel. Follow each presentation with a team standing ovation or saying. Your team can do a watermelon feed for another team on campus. This really works great if a varsity team does it for a junior varsity or freshmen team. Again, emphasize the Biblical principle that the greatest among you must be a servant!)

➤ A Quality use of a Waste of Time (As coaches we developed these nights to promote a fun, competitive atmosphere and to keep our players close and out of trouble in the off-season. The only rule is that it must be fun, competitive and not related to the sport they play. We created old school gym nights where we played floor hockey on one side of the gym and kick ball on the other. Elementary school gym team games were always a big hit. We also played no dribble basketball and ultimate Frisbee along with a game of capture the flag. We had video scavenger hunts and some games from "Whose line is it anyway". We found that the kids loved being together and looked forward to the nights. It also allowed us to foster an atmosphere where competition is going on and teachable moments are plentiful. Your brainstorming will create memories your players will never forget. By the way we didn't debrief the kids after the activities, we would pray or do the put up game.

"More is Caught than is Taught"

➤ Start another Legacy Builder Study group

➤ Mentor an athlete (As coaches we meet with our team leaders every week anyway to discuss who we are as a team, where we are going and how we are going to get there. Why not use that time to mentor them as a group and teach them how to compete and live with Biblical principles? We have written a study series very similar to the one you just completed, called *Winning God's Way!*. Get some books and block out 30 minutes a week. www.crosstrainingpub.com)

➤ Check out www.coachesministry.com for more ideas! And we would love to hear from you, please email us at rolson@fca.org.